A LIFEGUIDE BIBLE STUDY

MATTHEW

Being Discipled by Jesus

24 Studies in 2 Parts
for individuals or groups

Stephen & Jacalyn Eyre

With Notes for Leaders

INTERVARSITY PRESS
DOWNERS GROVE, ILLINOIS 60515

InterVarsity Press is the book-publishing division of InterVarsity Christian Fellowship, a student movement active on campus at hundreds of universities, colleges and schools of nursing. For information about local and regional activities, write Public Relations Dept., InterVarsity Christian Fellowship, 6400 Schroeder Rd., P.O. Box 7895, Madison, WI 53707-7895.

All Scripture quotations, unless otherwise indicated, are taken from the Holy Bible, New International Version. Copyright © 1973, 1978, International Bible Society. Used by permission of Zondervan Bible Publishers.

Cover photograph: David Singer

ISBN 0-8308-1003-X

Printed in the United States of America

18   17   16   15   14   13   12   11   10   9
99   98   97   96

Contents

Getting the Most
from LifeGuide Bible Studies

Many of us long to fill our minds and our lives with Scripture. We desire to be transformed by its message. LifeGuide Bible Studies are designed to be an exciting, and challenging way to do just that. They help us to be guided by God's Word in every area of life.

How They Work

LifeGuides have a number of distinctive features. Perhaps the most important is that they are *inductive* rather than *deductive*. They lead us to *discover* what the Bible says rather than *telling* us what it says.

They are also thought provoking. They help us to think about the meaning of the passage so that we can truly understand what the author is saying. The questions require more than one-word answers.

The studies are personal. Questions expose us to the promises, assurances, exhortations and challenges of God's Word. They are designed to allow the Scriptures to renew our minds so that we can be transformed by the Spirit of God. This is the ultimate goal of all Bible study.

The studies are versatile. They are designed for student, neighborhood and church groups. They are also effective for individual study.

How They're Put Together

LifeGuides also have a distinctive format. Each study need take no more than forty-five minutes in a group setting or thirty minutes in personal study—unless you choose to take more time.

The studies can be used within a quarter system in a church and fit well in a semester or trimester system on a college campus. If a guide has more than thirteen studies, it is divided into two or occasionally three parts of approximately twelve studies each.

LifeGuides use a workbook format. Space is provided for writing answers to each question. This is ideal for personal study and allows group members to prepare in advance for the discussion.

The studies also contain leader's notes. They show how to lead a group discussion, provide additional background information on certain questions, give helpful tips on group dynamics and suggest ways to deal with problems which may arise during the discussion. With such helps, someone with little or no experience can lead an effective study.

Suggestions for Individual Study

1. As you begin each study, pray that God will help you to understand and apply the passage to your life.

2. Read and reread the assigned passage to familiarize yourself with what the author is saying. You may want to read through the entire book prior to the first study to get an overview of its contents.

3. A good modern translation of the Bible, rather than the King James Version or a paraphrase, will give you the most help. The New International Version, the New American Standard Bible and the Revised Standard Version are all recommended. However, the questions in this guide are based on the New International Version.

4. Write your answers in the space provided in the study guide. This will help you to express your understanding of the passage clearly.

5. It might be good to have a Bible dictionary handy. Use it to look up any unfamiliar words, names or places.

Suggestions for Group Study

1. Come to the study prepared. Follow the suggestions for individual study mentioned above. You will find that careful preparation will greatly enrich your time spent in group discussion.

2. Participate in the discussion. The leader of your group will not be lecturing but encouraging the members to discuss what they have learned from the passage. The leader will be asking the questions that are found in this guide. Plan to share what God has taught you in your individual study.

3. Stick to the passage being studied. Your answers should be based on the verses which are the focus of the discussion and not on outside authorities such as commentaries or speakers.

4. Be sensitive to the other members of the group. Listen attentively when they share what they have learned. You may be surprised by their insights! Also, be affirming whenever you can. This will encourage some of the more hesitant members of the group to participate.

5. Be careful not to dominate the discussion. We are sometimes so eager to share what we have learned that we leave too little opportunity for others to respond. By all means participate! But allow others to also.

6. Expect God to teach you through the passage being discussed and through the other members. Pray for a profitable time together.

7. If you are the discussion leader, you will find additional suggestions for each study in the leader's notes. These are found at the back of the guide.

Introducing Matthew

What does it mean to be a disciple of Jesus Christ? How can we effectively disciple others? Christian bookstores are full of "how to" manuals which seek to answer these questions. The early church had a discipling manual too—the book of Matthew. It was written to teach us how to be a disciple of Jesus Christ and how to disciple others. Before looking at current discipling manuals, why not go back to one of the originals?

Discipleship is the application of Christian truth to the present. "What does God want me to do about this relationship?" "How can I deal with anxiety?" We need to know what God expects of us on a daily basis. Discipleship is a very practical matter.

Practical questions were a concern of Matthew as he wrote his book. Matthew was a tax collector, so he knew how important it was to be practical. A tax collector has to know things like how much tax you owe, where you pay and who is authorized to collect it. And when a tax is paid, it must be recorded exactly. Otherwise government authorities tend to become hostile. Very practical stuff.

Matthew draws on all his background as he writes. Your most important need as a disciple is to know what the Lord is like. Matthew will help you. Through his work you will get to know Jesus better as he responds to needy people, handles conflict and faces opposition. You will also see what Jesus is like as a King. How does he handle authority? What type of laws does he give? How does he provide for his subjects?

For your daily living you will discover how to handle anger and envy. You will learn how your faith can be strengthened, how to pray, how to grow in humility. You will gain insights into a biblical approach to evangelism. You will find out what attitudes the Lord thinks are important. And you will learn how to handle suffering and grief.

In short, a study of Matthew will help you become a better disciple and disciplemaker.

The content of Matthew will be covered by dividing it into two equal sections, 1:1—16:20 and 16:21—28:20. The first half is entitled "Discovering the King." It focuses on the identity and authority of Jesus. The second half is entitled "The Conflict and Victory of the King." It focuses on Jesus as he encounters opposition and persecution culminating in the cross and resurrection.

From beginning to end Matthew is an exciting and challenging Gospel. Get ready for an adventure!

Part 1
Discovering the King

Matthew 1:1—16:20

1
Discovering the King
Matthew 1:1—16:20

The French painter Georges Seurat painted with dots of color rather than brushstrokes. Up close the dots are meaningless, but from a distance they blend to form a beautiful painting.

Many times we look at only small portions of Scripture, chapters and verses, and see only dots. It is important to step back and see how the chapters and verses fit together to paint a picture.

An overview of Matthew also draws together seemingly isolated events and teachings into a meaningful whole. This study, which looks at chapters 1—16, will help you understand Matthew's purpose and style. As you are drawn deeper into the main plot, you will gain a greater appreciation for the gospel story.

1. As you look down at the landscape from an airplane, what features can you see that are not visible from the ground?

2. Matthew's theme statement is found in the last three verses of the last chapter (28:18-20). What is that theme?

3. Matthew wants us to see Jesus as a heavenly King. What attributes of a king do you see portrayed in these three verses?

How do you think this concern may have affected the way Matthew wrote his Gospel?

4. Quickly skim chapters 1—4. Matthew has recorded the things Jesus taught and commanded his disciples to teach others. What did Matthew feel a disciple should know about the beginnings of Jesus' ministry?

5. In chapters 5—7 we have a summary of the King's laws. As you skim these laws, what responses do you have?

What does Jesus expect of his disciples?

6. In chapters 8—9 the miracles of Jesus occupy a dominant part. In what ways are faith and authority a part of this section?

7. In the midst of widening conflict and controversy, Jesus reveals his true identity to the disciples (10:1—16:20). How does he do this in 14:1—16:20?

8. In 16:16 Peter's confession that Jesus is "the Christ, the Son of the living God," is the fruit of time and experience with Jesus. How did God bring you to the knowledge of Jesus as the Christ?

9. What do you hope to gain from studying Matthew?

2
In Search of the King
Matthew 1—2

Have you ever waited with anticipation for something only to find that when it came it was not what you wanted at all?

The long-awaited birth of the Messiah is recorded in Matthew 1—2. The nation of Israel waited for centuries for God's anointed King to be born. What a wonderful day that was to be. Jesus' birth, however, was not greeted with royal gladness by the nation and its leaders. Instead, there was intrigue and conflict. The political and religious establishment felt threatened by the coming of the Messiah. It was left to foreign leaders to welcome the newborn King.

1. Think of something you once strongly desired (a car, TV, stereo, a special relationship, or whatever). When you got it, did it fulfill your expectations? Explain why or why not.

2. Skim the genealogical record in 1:1-17. Considering Matthew's purpose to portray Jesus as a heavenly King, why would Matthew include a lineage at the very beginning of his book?

3. Read 1:18-25. Matthew highlights Jesus' birth in these verses. What do they tell us about his origin and destiny?

4. Read Matthew 2. In this chapter Matthew portrays Jesus' initial reception by the world. How does Jesus the heavenly King contrast with Herod the earthly king?

5. There are many traditions and myths in church history about the Magi which may or may not be true. But strictly from the information in this passage, what can we discover about them?

Describe the details of their search for Jesus.

6. How has knowing Jesus involved you in a search or journey?

7. How are the Magi different from the religious leaders in this passage?

8. Jesus was born during the time of King Herod (v. 1). From your reading of this chapter, what was Herod like?

9. On hearing of Jesus' birth from the searching Magi, Herod also begins a search for the newborn Christ. How does his search compare with that of the Magi?

10. The responses of the Magi and Herod are typical of the ways people respond to Jesus today. What factors might cause people to respond to Jesus in such radically different ways?

11. God is the unseen actor throughout the chapter. In what ways can we see his "behind the scenes" actions (vv. 6, 15, 18 and 23)?

12. The Magi not only found Jesus, they worshiped him and witnessed to the entire city of Jerusalem concerning his birth (vv. 2-3). In what ways has your search for the Lord resulted in worshiping him and telling others about him?

13. Spend time worshiping the King of kings. Then ask God to help you tell others about him.

3
Preparing for the King
Matthew 3:1-17

In ancient times the coming of a king required special preparation. A herald was sent ahead to prepare the road on which the king would be traveling. Holes were filled, rough places made smooth and crooked sections straightened.

The same thing happened in recent times when Queen Elizabeth II visited the Bahamas. In preparation for her coming, the roads she would be traveling on around the island were completely resurfaced.

In Matthew 3 John the Baptist is sent to prepare the way for the coming of the Lord. But his arrival required a very different kind of preparation.

1. Why do you think we go to such lengths preparing for visiting guests, dignitaries and heads of state?

2. Read Matthew 3. What are your initial impressions of John?

3. For Israel the desert was a place of both punishment and renewal (recall the wilderness wanderings). How does John's ministry convey both concepts (vv. 1-12)?

4. The religious leaders considered themselves children of Abraham (v. 9). According to verses 7-10, how were they abusing this privilege?

5. What are some ways that Christians today abuse their rights as children of God?

6. John calls us to produce "fruit in keeping with repentance" (v. 8). Give examples of the kind of fruit you think he has in mind.

7. Both John and Jesus have ministries of baptism (vv. 11-12). How are their baptisms similar and different?

8. Why do you think John was hesitant to baptize Jesus (vv. 13-14)?

9. What does Jesus' willingness to be baptized suggest about him (v. 15)?

In what ways was Jesus' baptism different from others?

10. What significance do you see in the dove and the voice from heaven at Jesus' baptism (vv. 16-17)?

11. The coming of Christ either demands repentance or brings judgment. In what ways do you need to better prepare for his return?

12. Think of people around you who have rough places or valleys in their lives. How can you help them smooth out the rough places or fill in the valleys in preparation for Jesus' coming?

4
The Beginning of the Kingdom

Matthew 4:1-25

Is it time yet?" "How much longer?" Those are the questions children ask repeatedly as Christmas approaches. It's hard on them (and their parents) to wait. But when Christmas day comes, it's full of fun and surprises. After weeks of waiting, we all get to open our new gifts.

The beginning of Jesus' ministry was like the coming of Christmas. After a long wait, the wrappings came off and the world got to see God's greatest gift.

1. All of us have experienced something new—starting a new job, going to a new school, moving to a new community. What did it feel like?

2. Read Matthew 4. Look over the entire chapter to discover the locations mentioned. What do they tell us about Jesus' ministry?

3. The prerequisite for Jesus' ministry was his ability to resist temptation. What can we discover about Jesus from his encounter with Satan (vv. 1-11)?

4. Look specifically at each temptation (vv. 3-4, 5-7, 8-10). What was Satan trying to accomplish by each of them?

5. What can we learn about temptation and how to resist it from Jesus' example?

6. Verses 12-17 describe the transition from testing to ministry. What do they tell us about Jesus' coming ministry?

7. How does Jesus demonstrate his message, "The kingdom of heaven is near," in verses 18-25?

8. One of Jesus' first functions as heavenly King is calling disciples. From verses 18-22 develop a brief definition of discipleship.

9. Discipleship for the first disciples meant leaving job and family and following Jesus wherever he went. How has discipleship affected your life?

10. In verses 23-25 Matthew gives us a summary statement of Jesus' initial public ministry. Describe the people who came looking for Jesus.

11. Imagine the excitement of the first disciples as they watched Jesus healing and teaching among the crowds. Put yourself in their place and describe how you would feel.

12. How does this chapter motivate you to follow Jesus and to be a "fisher of men"?

5
The Law of the King (Part 1)
Matthew 5:1–6:18

C. S. Lewis was once criticized for not caring for the Sermon on the Mount. He replied, "As to 'caring for' the Sermon on the Mount, if 'caring for' here means 'liking' or enjoying, I suppose no one 'cares for' it. Who can *like* being knocked flat on his face by a sledge hammer? I can hardly imagine a more deadly spiritual condition than that of a man who can read that passage with tranquil pleasure."*

Lewis was right. Studying the Sermon on the Mount can be a devastating experience. It exposes the depth of our sin and the shallowness of our commitment. But the pain it inflicts is meant to heal not destroy us. In fact, the Sermon on the Mount could be called the Christian's job description. It is the most complete summary we have of Jesus' ethical expectations for his followers. Throughout church history it has been a helpful guide and a convicting challenge.

---

1. Have you ever had a job or a task in which you did not know what was expected of you? How would a job description have helped?

2. Read Matthew 5. The beatitudes describe the qualities Jesus desires in each of his disciples (vv. 3-12). Give a brief definition of each quality.

3. What is attractive about the blessings Jesus promises those who have these qualities (vv. 3-12)?

4. Jesus compares his followers to salt and light (vv. 13-16). What do these metaphors suggest about our role in society?

5. In the rest of chapter 5 Jesus discusses various misconceptions we might have about the Law (Old Testament Scriptures). Why do you think that Jesus stresses that he did not come to abolish the Law (vv. 17-20)?

6. How does Jesus' teaching on murder and adultery (vv. 21-30) differ from the traditional understanding?

7. In verses 31-37 Jesus provides instructions on divorce and oaths (legal relationships). How does his teaching confront tradition?

8. How does Jesus want us to respond to evil people and our enemies (vv. 38-47)?

9. Verse 48 summarizes the essence of what Jesus has been saying. How does this verse challenge spiritual complacency?

10. Read Matthew 6:1-18. What do we learn about proper and improper motives from Jesus' examples about giving, praying and fasting?

11. Why are our motives just as important as our religious acts?

12. What is your impression of Jesus after studying the first half of his sermon?

God in the Dock (Grand Rapids, Mich.: Eerdmans, 1970), pp. 181-82.

6
The Law of the King (Part 2)
Matthew 6:19—7:29

J im Elliot, a missionary killed by the Auca Indians, once wrote: "He is no fool who gives what he cannot keep to gain what he cannot lose." His words echo this portion of the Sermon on the Mount. Jesus asks us to choose between two treasures, two masters, two roads and two destinies. But he clearly explains why following him is the only wise choice.

1. Why are earthly treasures often more tempting than heavenly ones?

2. Read Matthew 6:19-34. In verses 19-24 Jesus talks about treasures, eyes and masters. What common themes tie these verses together?

3. Worry is a dominant theme in verses 25-34. How can we escape worrying about such things as food and clothes?

4. What does it mean to seek first God's kingdom and righteousness (v. 33)?

How might this affect our lives in practical ways?

5. Read Matthew 7:1-29. What is the difference between judging others and being properly discerning (vv. 1-6)?

6. In what ways have you seen relationships hurt by Christians judging each other?

7. How should our knowledge of the Father affect our prayers (vv. 7-11)?

8. In the final section of the Sermon (vv. 13-27) Jesus talks about narrow and wide gates, good and bad trees, and wise and foolish builders. How do these three metaphors work together to make a common point?

What reasons are we given for obeying Jesus' teaching?

9. We are cautioned about false prophets and false followers in verses 15-23. What distinguishes genuine prophets and followers from false ones?

10. Putting Jesus' words in practice is the way to build a lasting foundation against the day of judgment (vv. 24-27). What will the practice of Jesus' Sermon require of you?

7
The Powers of the King
Matthew 8:1—9:34

Someone once commented about a U.S. president: "I don't know where he is going, but I sure like the way he leads."

Leaders must demonstrate authority. But wise leaders know they must not abuse their authority. They know people follow leaders who also demonstrate integrity and compassion.

In the Sermon on the Mount Jesus impressed the crowd with his authoritative teaching. In chapters 8 and 9 he demonstrates that he is a worthy King, one in whom we can safely put our trust.

---

1. Think of someone in your life whom you respect. Why do you respect that person?

---

2. Read Matthew 8:1-22. In chapters 8—9 Jesus' miracles occur in three groups, followed by a response or reaction. Briefly describe how Jesus demonstrates his authority in verses 1-22.

3. Lepers were outcasts in Jewish society and were required to shout "Unclean, unclean!" wherever they went. What impresses you about Jesus' encounter with the man in verses 1-4?

4. Look at the centurion's response to Jesus (vv. 5-13). Why is Jesus pleased?

5. In verses 18-22 Jesus begins to attract would-be followers. What do these verses teach us about the cost and urgency of following him?

6. Read Matthew 8:23—9:17. What do we learn about the extent of Jesus' authority in this section?

7. The disciples' fear of the furious storm seems natural (8:23-27). Why do you think Jesus views it as a lack of faith?

8. After what had happened to the demon-possessed men, why do you think the townspeople pleaded with Jesus to leave their region (vv. 28-34)?

9. What is the relationship between Jesus' claim to have authority to forgive sins and his healing of the paralytic (9:1-8)?

10. In verses 9-17 Jesus compares himself to a doctor and a bridegroom. Then he discusses garments and wineskins. What do these illustrations teach us about his ministry?

11. Read Matthew 9:18-34. How do people respond to Jesus in this section?

12. Look back over chapters 8—9. How does Jesus want us to respond to his power and authority?

13. How can a knowledge of Jesus' power and authority strengthen our faith?

8
The Messengers of the King

Matthew 9:35—11:30

During the late 1800s a wealthy philanthropist decided to give away all his money. He announced he would give five hundred dollars to anyone with a legitimate need. The response was overwhelming! People lined up day after day to receive their gift.

The gospel is a priceless treasure. But as we offer it to people their response is not always enthusiastic. In this passage Jesus warns us about those who oppose his message and his messengers. But he also encourages us as we reach out to blind and needy people.

1. Have you ever known someone who seemed to like you only for what you could give them? What did it feel like?

2. Read Matthew 9:35—11:1. How and why does Jesus demonstrate compassion for the crowds (9:35-38)?

In what ways are people today similar to those Jesus describes?

3. As a result of his compassion for the crowds, Jesus sends out the twelve (vv. 1-15). Describe their mission.

4. Jesus warns the disciples that their compassionate ministry will not be warmly received (vv. 16-25). What will they experience?

5. In verses 26-33 Jesus prepares his present and future disciples for opposition. Why shouldn't we be afraid of those who oppose us?

6. How might following Christ strain our family relationships and loyalties?

7. What does Jesus promise to those who are receptive to our message (vv. 40-42)?

8. Read Matthew 11:2-30. What is the point of John's question and Jesus' reply (vv. 2-6)?

9. What do verses 7-19 tell us about John and those who heard his message?

10. In verses 20-30 Jesus denounces some and offers a warm invitation to others. What causes his denunciations?

What is the nature of Jesus' invitation?

11. In what ways have you found rest in your life by coming to Jesus?

12. What have you learned about Jesus and the nature of discipleship from this study?

9
The Leaders and the King

Matthew 12:1-50

P ower over people is not easily shared. Wars have been fought, people assassinated and elections rigged in order to gain or maintain power.

The leaders of Israel were becoming concerned over the growing reputation and following of Jesus. Like ripples in a pool of water, the ministry of Jesus and his disciples continued to have a widening impact on the Jewish nation. If Jesus' followers became too numerous, the leaders would end up losing their positions of authority. In Matthew 12 they formulate a strategy to discredit him.

1. How would you feel if untrue rumors were being spread around about you?

2. Read Matthew 12. How would you describe the mood or atmosphere of this chapter?

3. Consider the ways that religious leaders attacked Jesus in verses 1-14. What was their strategy?

4. Jesus answers the Pharisees' first accusation by making three references to Scripture (vv. 3-8). How do these passages prove the innocence of his disciples?

5. As you compare the Pharisees' second accusation against Jesus (v. 10) with their own response (v. 14), what irony do you see?

6. Throughout verses 1-14 how does Jesus' attitude toward people and Scripture differ from that of the Pharisees?

How can Jesus' example guide our own interpretation and use of Scripture?

7. Notice the startling contrast between the religious leaders' attitude toward Jesus and God's attitude (vv. 15-21). How do they differ?

8. In order to discredit the idea that Jesus is the Messiah, the Pharisees charge that his power over demons comes from the prince of demons (v. 24). How does Jesus refute this claim (vv. 25-37)?

9. Why will the men of Nineveh and the Queen of the South condemn "this generation" (vv. 38-42)?

10. In verses 43-45 Jesus tells the Pharisees and teachers of the law a story. What does it reveal about them?

11. Look back over chapter 12. What factors led to the hardness and unbelief of the Pharisees and teachers of the law?

How can we avoid being like them?

10
The Parables of the King
Matthew 13:1-58

Crowds are fickle. One moment they follow with enthusiasm, the next they turn hostile and angry.

In Matthew 13 Jesus speaks to a mixed and fickle crowd. Some are hungry to hear his message. Others are suspicious and hostile. In this setting Jesus begins to speak in parables. These stories test our spiritual sight and hearing. They also expose the condition of our hearts.

1. Some people are hooked on mystery novels. How do mysteries keep people reading?

2. Read Matthew 13. What initial impressions do you have of the kingdom of heaven?

3. According to the parable of the sower, what responses does Jesus expect as he preaches his message of the kingdom (vv. 1-9, 18-23)?

4. In verse 10 the disciples ask Jesus why he speaks to the people in parables. Explain his reply (vv. 11-17).

5. Wheat and weeds look similar until the harvest. How does this parable explain God's delayed judgment of the wicked (vv. 24-30, 36-43)?

6. What do the parables of the mustard seed and yeast suggest about the way the kingdom grows (vv. 31-35)?

7. Reflect on the parables we have looked at so far. What practical implications do they have for our evangelism?

8. What do the parables of the hidden treasure and the pearl teach us about the value of the kingdom (vv. 44-46)?

9. This chapter concludes with a visit to Jesus' hometown (vv. 53-58). How do the people there compare with those described in verses 13-15?

10. Jesus wants his disciples to understand the parables. How have they enlarged your understanding of the kingdom of heaven?

11. Jesus also wants us to respond to what we have heard and understood. Throughout this chapter, what types of responses does he desire?

12. Ask the Lord to help you respond to him in these ways.

11
The Revelation of the King (Part 1)
Matthew 14:1-36

Crises are uncomfortable. They force us to make painful decisions, even when we don't want to decide. In Matthew 14 Jesus places the disciples in tough situations where they must act on what they have learned about him. The focus shifts from parables about the kingdom to the identity of the King.

1. Teachers use tests during our school years. But tests are not limited to school; God also uses tests throughout our lives. In what ways do tests help us learn?

2. Read Matthew 14. In verses 1-2 Herod speculates about Jesus' identity. What led him to believe that Jesus is John the Baptist (vv. 3-12)?

3. Describe the circumstances, the setting and the people present during the feeding of the five thousand (vv. 13-21).

How is this a test for the disciples?

4. Herod and Jesus, the two kings in this passage, both serve banquets. What does each king's banquet reveal about his character and authority?

5. Imagine you are with the anxious disciples in the boat (vv. 22-26). Describe what you would see, hear and feel.

6. How is Peter's trying experience on the water a vivid picture of faith and doubt (vv. 28-31)?

7. When are you most tempted to take your eyes off the Lord and to sink in doubt?

8. In verse 33 the disciples worship Jesus and declare, "Truly you are the Son of God." What do you see in this incident that leads you to worship Jesus?

How can these things help you to trust Jesus the next time you are tempted to doubt?

9. Through these puzzling experiences with Jesus the disciples come to confess that he is the Son of God. What experiences have helped you understand more about the Lord?

10. How does the recognition of the crowds in verses 34-36 compare with the recognition of the disciples in verse 33?

11. Spend a few minutes worshiping Jesus, the Son of God.

12
The Revelation of the King (Part 2)
Matthew 15:1—16:20

Eureka! A word to describe a sudden insight. What a relief and pleasure when something we have not quite understood becomes clear to us.

In this section of Matthew the disciples come to a supernatural understanding of Jesus. What they thought they knew becomes a new and deeper knowledge. Peter, speaking for the disciples, declares who Jesus really is.

Peter's words bring us to the climax of the first half of Matthew.

1. The climax of a story is packed with emotion. What feelings have you experienced when reaching the climax of an exciting story?

2. Read Matthew 15. Top religious leaders from Jerusalem oppose Jesus by attacking the disciples (vv. 1-2). What is their complaint, and what does it suggest about Jesus?

3. How does Jesus respond to their accusation (vv. 3-20)?

4. Are there religious practices in your life which are in danger of becoming outward, empty forms? Explain.

How can you avoid this tendency?

5. How would you account for the unusual interaction between Jesus, the woman and the disciples (vv. 21-28)?

6. Observe the similarities and differences between the feeding of the four thousand (vv. 29-39) and the feeding of the five thousand (14:13-21). What do these banquets show us about Jesus?

7. Read Matthew 16:1-20. After Jesus heals the sick and feeds the four thousand, the religious leaders ask him for a sign from heaven (v. 1). Why do you think Jesus resists them (vv. 2-4)?

8. In verses 5-12 the disciples misunderstand Jesus' allusion to yeast. How is their misunderstanding related to a lack of faith?

9. In verses 5-12 the disciples couldn't even grasp a simple figure of speech. How then does Peter have enough insight to confess that Jesus is the Christ, the Son of God (vv. 13-17)?

10. How will Peter's confession of Jesus as the Christ, the Son of God unlock the entrance to the kingdom of heaven for others (vv. 18-20)?

11. Jesus' question to Peter is one that everyone will have to respond to at some point. Who do you say Jesus is, and why?

Part 2
The Rejection and Resurrection of the King

Matthew 16:21—28:20

1
The Conflict and Victory of the King

Matthew 16:21—28:20

W hat's the point?" Have you ever listened to someone giving detail after detail of some past experience? Initially you were interested in the story, but somehow the point seemed to get lost beneath all the talk.

Matthew gives us lots of details about Jesus ministry, but he has a point to make. Don't get lost in the details. This overview of the last half of Matthew helps us to see his main point and to put the details into perspective.

In the first half of Matthew we were introduced to Jesus and his kingdom. We read about his compassionate teaching and healing. In the last half we will see that Jesus' work went far beyond teaching and healing. At great cost to himself he confronts the powers of darkness and becomes a mighty victor and deliverer.

---

1. Occasionally we meet someone who inspires us. Recall someone whom you have admired and describe something about them you found inspiring.

---

2. Briefly look over 16:21—17:27. How is the suffering and glory of Jesus' mission displayed in this section?

---

3. Chapters 18—20 are similar in many ways to the Sermon on the Mount. Read through them quickly, looking for ways the disciples can become great in the kingdom.

4. Describe the ways that Jesus demonstrates his kingly authority as he occupies the temple and the capital city of Israel in chapters 21 and 22.

5. Jesus continues to display kingly authority in chapter 23. What can you discover about the reasons Jesus judges the religious leaders?

6. Jesus wants his disciples to anticipate the future and final coming of his kingdom. How does he create a sense of expectation in chapters 24 and 25?

7. The final events of Jesus' earthly life come to a climax in chapters 26 and 27. As you look over those events, what impressions do you have?

8. Ultimate victory! In chapter 28 Jesus triumphs over suffering, conflict and death. Put yourself in the disciples' place. What might you be feeling?

9. Reflecting on what you have just seen in the last half of Matthew, what have you learned about the Lord Jesus? About discipleship?

2
The Work of the King
Matthew 16:21—17:27

One of the rules of good management is "No surprises." While surprises can be fun, they can also be upsetting. Good corporate leadership seeks to eliminate surprises so that everything runs according to plan.

Now that the disciples have been with Jesus for a while he must prepare them for the true nature of his kingdom. They are shocked at the cost of his mission and his requirements for discipleship.

1. Recall an unpleasant surprise you received. How did you handle it?

2. Read Matthew 16:21—17:13. What were some of the surprises the disciples received?

3. Jesus' statements do not fit the Jewish expectation of a conquering Messiah (vv. 21-22). In what specific ways are they different?

4. Peter and Jesus seem to be at cross purposes in verses 22-23. Why do you think Jesus addresses Peter as Satan?

5. What does Jesus reveal about the cost and rewards of following him (vv. 24-28)?

6. How might the transfiguration be a fulfillment of Jesus' puzzling statement in 16:28?

7. What would the disciples learn about Jesus by his transformed appearance, his conversation with Moses and Elijah, and the voice from heaven (17:1-8)?

How might this help resolve their confusion about Jesus' impending death?

8. Having just seen Elijah on the mountain, the disciples are puzzled about his future ministry (v. 10). In what sense was Elijah's ministry fulfilled by John the Baptist (vv. 11-13)?

9. How has following Jesus produced times of confusion for you?

10. Read 17:14-27. Describe your impression of Jesus as he confronts the powerless disciples.

11. As a result of their powerlessness, what do the disciples learn about faith?

12. We don't always understand life from a heavenly perspective. How can this passage reorient our thinking?

3
Life in the Kingdom (Part 1)
Matthew 18:1-35

Who is greatest in the kingdom of God? How can a subject of the kingdom earn true wealth? These questions dominate the thoughts of the disciples as they approach Jerusalem. They are also important questions for us. How we answer them will directly affect the quality of our discipleship.

1. In what ways are people of status and social standing treated differently from others?

2. Read Matthew 18. The disciples want to know who is the greatest in the kingdom of heaven (v. 1). How does Jesus' appeal to little children answer their question (vv. 2-5)?

3. Children have little status in the eyes of adults. How can we assume the status of children in our circle of friends and coworkers?

4. Spiritually speaking, the "little ones" are those who humble themselves ("become like little children") and believe in Jesus. What is Jesus' attitude toward those who cause the little ones to sin (vv. 6-7)?

5. How does Jesus graphically illustrate the importance of dealing with sin in our lives (vv. 8-9)?

6. How do verses 10-14 further emphasize the value Jesus places on his "little ones"?

7. How should the value Jesus places on his "little ones" affect the way we view ourselves and other believers?

8. Greatness in the kingdom is also dependent on living a life of forgiveness and mercy. What guidelines does Jesus give for dealing with those who sin against us (vv. 15-20)?

Why is each step in this procedure important?

9. Forgiving someone once does not always guarantee he or she will not offend us again. How can the parable of the unmerciful servant help us to keep on forgiving (vv. 21-35)?

10. How does this chapter challenge the world's concept of greatness?

How does it challenge your own ideas of value and greatness?

4
Life in the Kingdom (Part 2)
Matthew 19:1—20:34

W hat is really important to you? What makes you feel important? Money? Success? Recognition? These are common answers. The values that Jesus teaches, however, have little to do with such things. In the previous study we learned that to be great in the kingdom we must become "small." In this study we will see how the values of the kingdom conflict with the world's approach to wealth and leadership.

1. What does it mean to be successful in our culture?

2. Read Matthew 19. How do Jesus' teachings on divorce and remarriage contrast with the values and practices of our culture (vv. 1-12)?

3. Children are brought to Jesus in verses 13-15. The disciples' response demonstrates they have not yet learned the meaning of greatness. Why do you think this is so hard to grasp?

4. In verses 16-22 a young man struggles between choosing wealth or eternal life. Why do you think Jesus required him to choose?

5. Wealth was considered a sign of God's favor and a reward for righteous living. How does Jesus challenge this concept (vv. 23-26)?

6. What wealth does Jesus offer those who follow him (vv. 27-30)?

How have you experienced what Jesus describes in verse 29?

7. Read Matthew 20. What does the parable of the workers teach us about greatness and wealth in the kingdom of God (vv. 1-16)?

8. In light of Jesus' statement about his impending death (vv. 17-19), how does the mother's request seem inappropriate (vv. 20-24)?

9. In what ways is Jesus a model of the values he teaches in verses 25-28?

10. How might conflict among Christians be reduced if we followed Jesus' teaching and example?

11. How does Jesus' interaction with the two blind men illustrate the values he has just taught?

12. In what ways has Jesus' teaching on greatness and wealth (Mt 18—20) challenged you?

5
The King Occupies His Capital
Matthew 21:1-27

It is fashionable to believe in Jesus. Surveys reveal that millions profess to be Christians. Celebrities claim miraculous, overnight conversions. Politicians boast they are "born again." Religion has become big business.

In Matthew 21 Jesus' popularity reaches its zenith. In the midst of public acclamation he occupies Jerusalem, the capital of the Jewish nation. His clash with the religious leaders reveals the difference between genuine faith and empty profession.

1. What is your response to reports that Jesus' popularity is increasing in our culture?

2. Read Matthew 21:1-27. Excitement is building and emotions are intense. What words or phrases communicate something of the electrifying atmosphere?

3. How do you think the disciples felt as they witnessed the excitement of the crowd and saw Jesus riding on a donkey, fulfilling a prophecy about the Messiah?

4. What different perceptions does the crowd have of Jesus (vv. 9-11)?

5. What is your impression of Jesus in verses 1-11?

6. Jesus clears the temple in verses 12-17. How does the condition of the temple contrast with what God intended?

7. A fig tree with leaves usually had fruit. How does Jesus' cursing of the fig tree relate to his clearing the temple (vv. 18-22)?

8. Why do you think Jesus answers the religious leaders with a question (vv. 23-27)?

9. How does Jesus' encounter with the Pharisees illustrate the danger of not responding to the light God gives us?

10. Identify one area in which your actions need to be more consistent with your beliefs.

11. What impresses you most about Jesus' leadership style in this passage?

6
The King Silences the Opposition
Matthew 21:28—22:46

Confrontation is never easy. Yet there are times when the situation demands it. The religious leaders refused to acknowledge that Jesus was God's Messiah sent to rule. Skillfully, Jesus seeks to expose their hardness of heart and bring them to repentance. They respond, not in repentance, but by plotting a trap for him.

1. From time to time we all have been involved in confrontations. How do you feel in these situations?

2. Questions and parables seem to be a focus of Matthew 21:28—22:46. Skim the whole passage. What motives seem to be behind the questions and the parables?

3. Read Matthew 21:28—22:14. What does the parable of the two sons reveal about the chief priests and the elders (vv. 28-32)?

4. How can we avoid the errors of the two sons—especially the second?

5. How does the parable of the tenants illustrate the character of the Father, the Son and the religious leaders (vv. 33-46)?

6. How is the kingdom of heaven like the banquet described in 22:1-14?

7. Read Matthew 22:15-46. Paying taxes to Caesar was an explosive issue— the Herodians approved of it, but the Pharisees opposed it. How might Jesus' ministry have been discredited by choosing one side or the other (vv. 15-22)?

8. What guidance does Jesus give us for fulfilling our obligations to God and the government?

9. In verses 23-28 the Sadducees tell Jesus a story designed to refute the resurrection. How does the story illustrate their ignorance of Scripture and God's power (vv. 29-33)?

10. Love was the foundation of the Old Testament law (vv. 34-40). Why do you think we have so much trouble equating God's laws with love?

11. Jesus poses a dilemma to the Pharisees that silences them: "How can the Christ be both the son of David and his Lord?" (vv. 41-46). What does this paradox reveal about the Lord?

12. How can these accounts of Jesus in conflict strengthen our faith in him?

7
The King Condemns the Rebels

Matthew 23:1-39

Influence is a powerful force. Those who influence others are able to change minds and to direct actions.

The religious leaders in Israel possessed the power of influence. After they decided to oppose Jesus, they tried to lead others to do the same. In Matthew 23 Jesus condemns them pointblank. They should have been the first to enter the kingdom of God because of their knowledge of Scripture and their standing in the Jewish community. Because they refused, Jesus calls them to judgment. This passage exposes the guilt of those who do not practice what they preach.

1. Give examples of leaders who have used their influence for good or bad.

2. Read Matthew 23. What words would you use to describe the teachers of the law and the Pharisees?

3. What attitude does Jesus teach the people to have toward the religious leaders, and why (vv. 1-4)?

4. Compare the motives of the religious leaders (vv. 5-7) with the motives and attitudes Jesus requires of his followers (vv. 8-12).

5. As followers of Jesus, how can we avoid these pitfalls of the religious leaders?

6. Jesus pronounces seven woes (judgments) against the teachers of the law and the Pharisees (vv. 13-32). Summarize each one.

7. Why do you think it was necessary to condemn the religious leaders before the whole community?

8. Jesus condemns the religious leaders for confusing inward and outward righteousness (vv. 25-28). In what ways are we inclined to do that today?

9. The entire generation to whom Jesus is speaking is held accountable for the "righteous blood shed in all previous generations" (vv. 33-36). Why do you think they received such a terrible sentence?

10. What responses do you have as you observe Jesus as a judge?

11. In the midst of this overwhelming condemnation, how is the tender compassion of Jesus also evident (vv. 33-39)?

12. What warnings and hope does this chapter offer us?

8
The Return of the King
Matthew 24:1-51

We all want to be safe and secure. Yet many things can threaten our security—losing our job, our income, our health, our loved ones. Our ability to handle these threats will depend on the source of our security.

Matthew 24 focuses on the destruction of Jerusalem and the return of Christ. The true issue of Christ's return is not the "hows" or "whens" that fascinate us. Rather we must learn to live in the present in light of the future. We must learn the true source of our security.

1. What gives you a sense of security?

2. Read Matthew 24:1-51. Both the temple's size and symbolism gave the Israelites a sense of security. When Jesus tells the disciples the temple will be destroyed (vv. 1-2), how do you think they feel?

3. Following Jesus' statement about the temple's destruction, the disciples ask two questions (vv. 1-3). Look through chapter 24, briefly noting ways that Jesus answers these questions.

4. Throughout history people have set dates for Christ's return and have been mistaken. What events might deceive the disciples into thinking the end is at hand (vv. 4-8)?

5. Before the end comes, what dangers will believers face, and how are we to handle them (vv. 9-14)?

6. In 167 B.C. Antiochus Epiphanes attacked Jerusalem and set up a pagan altar in the temple—an event which anticipates "the abomination that causes desolation" spoken of by Jesus (v. 15). What occurs in the aftermath of this abomination (vv. 15-22)?

7. In A.D. 70 the Roman general Titus captured Jerusalem and destroyed the temple. Do you think verses 15-22 refer to this event or to events immediately preceding the return of Christ—or both? Explain.

8. Few of us have ever faced deadly peril for our faith. What types of pressure do you face for your faith in Christ?

9. How will we be able to distinguish false Christs from the true (vv. 23-31)?

10. The time of Christ's coming is discussed in verses 32-41. What can be known about the timing?

What can't be known?

11. How do the parables of the thief and the wise and wicked servants (vv. 42-51) emphasize the importance of living in light of Christ's return?

12. In what ways do you have need of greater watchfulness and perseverance?

9
Preparation for the King's Return

Matthew 25:1-46

Accountability can be uncomfortable and inconvenient. Our desires and preferences are subject to the demands of another. Most of us would prefer to do things our own way. A rule of thumb in management is that people don't do what you expect; they do what you inspect.

Jesus is coming back to inspect our lives. He holds us accountable for how we conduct ourselves in his absence. In Matthew 25 he urges us to prepare for his coming.

1. Have you ever been in a situation where your work did not meet up to standards when it was reviewed or inspected? How did it affect you?

2. Read Matthew 25. How does the parable of the ten virgins illustrate the need to prepare for the groom's delayed return (vv. 1-13)?

3. How can we prepare ourselves for Jesus return?

4. A talent was a vast sum of money. In the parable of the talents, what were the master's expectations of his servants (vv. 14-30)?

5. How does the master demonstrate his approval or disapproval?

6. What resources and responsibilities has Jesus given you?

How can you handle them in a good and faithful manner?

7. In the parable of the sheep and the goats, identify the King, the sheep, the goats and the "brothers" of the King (vv. 31-46).

8. What criteria does the King use to separate the sheep from the goats?

9. As you reflect on the parables in this chapter, what similarities and differences can you find between the main characters?

10. According to Jesus' teaching in this chapter, what should we be doing until he returns?

11. How should the material in this chapter affect your current priorities?

10
The Betrayal of the King
Matthew 26:1-75

On the drizzly day of October 16, 1555, Hugh Latimer and Nicholas Ridley, two influential English reformers, were tied to the stake and bundles of sticks were piled at their feet. The crowd strained to hear what the two men were saying. Would they recant or would they persist in dying as heretics?

As the executioner pushed a torch into the wood, Latimer said, "Be of good comfort, Master Ridley, and play the man; we shall this day light such a candle, by God's grace, in England, as I trust shall never be put out."

Suffering and temptation reveal the quality of our discipleship. Nowhere is this more evident than in Matthew 26 as we move into the climax of the book. Both Jesus and his disciples face a time of severe testing. The way they respond to these tests can be an encouragement and a warning to us.

1. Have you ever been tempted to stop following Christ? Explain.

2. Read Matthew 26:1-35. How do verses 1-16 set the stage for Jesus' betrayal and death?

3. In verses 17-30 Jesus celebrates the Passover with his disciples. How is this occasion both ominous and hopeful?

4. Why do you think Jesus tells his disciples that one of them will betray him, Peter will disown him, and the others will fall away (vv. 21-25, 31-35)?

5. When have you been confronted with the weakness of your commitment to the Lord?

6. Read Matthew 26:36-75. What insights can we discover about Jesus during his time in Gethsemane (vv. 36-45)?

7. Jesus exhorts the disciples to "watch and pray so that you will not fall into temptation" (v. 41). What temptations were they about to face?

8. Jesus' betrayal comes at the hand of one of his own disciples (vv. 47-50). As you look over the role of Judas in this chapter, why do you think the religious leaders used him?

9. Twice during his arrest Jesus states that the Scriptures are being fulfilled (vv. 54, 56). What significance would this have for those who heard him: the disciples, the crowd and the religious leaders?

10. Why do you think Jesus remained silent during the first part of his trial (vv. 57-63)?

11. In answer to the high priest's question (v. 63), Jesus declares that he is the Christ (alluding to Dan 7:13-14). Describe the immediate—and ultimate—impact of Jesus' words on those present (vv. 65-68)?

12. Peter's attempt to be courageous turns to cowardice (vv. 69-75). What role do fear and faith occupy in his denial of the Lord?

13. Both Jesus and the disciples faced temptation in this chapter. How can Jesus' example and the disciples' failures help us to withstand temptation and testing?

11
The Crucifixion of the King
Matthew 27:1-66

My God, my God, why have you forsaken me?
Why are you so far from saving me, so far from the words of my groaning?
O my God, I cry out by day, but you do not answer, by night, and am not silent" (Ps 22:1-2).

Do you ever feel that God is absent when you need him most? You pray but receive no answer. You cry but no one seems to care.

Matthew 27 records the judgment and execution of Jesus. As Pilate and the religious leaders condemn, mock and crucify God's Son, God himself seems strangely absent. Yet to those who have eyes to see, his presence and power are unmistakable.

1. Recall a time when you felt as though God were absent when you needed him. How did you handle it?

2. Read Matthew 27:1-31. After the religious leaders hand Jesus over to Pilate, Judas feels remorse (vv. 1-5). How is remorse different from repentance?

3. Jesus stands before Pilate in verses 11-26. How and why does Pilate seek to avoid sentencing Jesus?

4. Social pressure affected Pilate's ultimate response to Jesus. In what ways has social pressure affected your relationship to Jesus?

5. The soldiers viciously mock Jesus in verses 27-31. What does their mockery reveal about their knowledge of Jesus?

6. Read Matthew 27:32-66. As Jesus hangs on the cross, he is repeatedly mocked and insulted (vv. 32-44). How do these insults reveal the spiritual choices these people have made?

7. As death begins to engulf him, Jesus cries out to God (vv. 45-46). What does his cry, and the overshadowing darkness, reveal about his relationship to the Father during this torment?

8. As the centurion witnesses the strange events surrounding Jesus' death, he exclaims, "Surely he was the Son of God!" (v. 54). What clues do the unusual events in verses 45-56 provide for understanding his divinity?

9. Observe the role Jesus' followers play during the events of his crucifixion and burial (vv. 55-61). How do you think they felt?

10. Notice the final measures the chief priests and Pharisees take to insure that their victory over Jesus is complete (vv. 62-66). What do you think they were feeling?

11. This chapter is filled with irony. Satan's triumph is actually his defeat. Christ's "defeat" is actually his triumph. How should this challenge our views about the way God works in our lives?

12
The Resurrection of the King
Matthew 28:1-20

Victory requires proclamation! Once a battle has been won, it's time to spread the word. Matthew 28 focuses on the messengers of Jesus' resurrection—the angel tells the women, the women tell the disciples, the disciples tell the nations, even the guards tell the religious leaders.

As Matthew concludes his Gospel, we are invited to join with those who throughout history have been witnesses and messengers of Jesus, the victorious resurrected Lord.

---

1. Who first brought you the message of Jesus and the challenge of discipleship?

---

2. Read Matthew 28, observing the people who are involved. How does each respond to the appearances of Jesus?

3. The angel is the first messenger of the resurrection (vv. 2-7). What is the significance of his appearance and words?

4. Consider the mission of the women (vv. 1-9). How does it undergo a radical change?

5. The Roman guard and the Jewish leaders are confronted with a miracle. How do they respond and why?

6. What keeps people today from believing that Jesus is the resurrected Lord?

7. The resurrection of Jesus affected everyone associated with it. How has the resurrection affected your life?

8. Consider the false story of the religious leaders and guards (vv. 11-15). Why doesn't it make sense to say that the disciples stole Jesus' body?

9. How would the false stories circulated by the guards hinder the disciples as they began their ministry?

10. The disciples go to Galilee where they meet with Jesus. Describe the commission he gives to them and us (vv. 16-20).

How would this commission sound to the Jewish disciples?

11. How does Jesus equip them and future disciples to carry out his commission?

12. As you conclude this study of Matthew, how can you be more involved in making disciples and fulfilling the Great Commission?

13. Pray that God will help you to be faithful to this task.

Leader's Notes

Leading a Bible discussion can be a rewarding experience. But it can also be *scary*—especially if you've never done it before. If this is your feeling, you're in good company. When God asked Moses to lead the Israelites out of Egypt, he replied, "O Lord, please send someone else to do it!" (Ex 4:13).

When Solomon became king of Israel, he felt the task was far beyond his abilities. "I am only a little child and do not know how to carry out my duties. . . . Who is able to govern this great people of yours?" (1 Kings 3:7, 9).

When God called Jeremiah to be a prophet, he replied, "Ah, Sovereign LORD, . . . I do not know how to speak; I am only a child" (Jer 1:6).

The list goes on. The apostles were "unschooled, ordinary men" (Acts 4:13). Timothy was young, frail and frightened. Paul's "thorn in the flesh" made him feel weak. But God's response to all of his servants—including you—is essentially the same: "My grace is sufficient for you" (2 Cor 12:9). Relax. God helped these people in spite of their weaknesses, and he can help you in spite of your feelings of inadequacy.

There is another reason why you should feel encouraged. Leading a Bible discussion is not difficult if you follow certain guidelines. You don't need to be an expert on the Bible or a trained teacher. The suggestions listed below should enable you to effectively and enjoyably fulfill your role as leader.

Preparing to Lead

1. Ask God to help you understand and apply the passage to your own life. Unless this happens, you will not be prepared to lead others. Pray too for the various members of the group. Ask God to give you an enjoyable and profitable time together studying his Word.

2. As you begin each study, read and reread the assigned Bible passage to familiarize yourself with what the author is saying. To get an overview you may want to read through the entire book prior to the first study.

3. This study guide is based on the New International Version of the Bible. It will help you and the group if you use this translation as the basis for your study and discussion. Encourage others to use the NIV also, but allow them the freedom to use whatever translation they prefer.

4. Carefully work through each question in the study. Spend time in meditation and reflection as you formulate your answers.

5. Write your answers in the space provided in the study guide. This will help you to express your understanding of the passage clearly.

6. It might help you to have a Bible dictionary handy. Use it to look up any unfamiliar words, names or places.

7. Once you have finished your own study of the passage, familiarize yourself with the leader's notes for the study you are leading. These are designed to help you in several ways. First, they tell you the purpose the study guide author had in mind while writing the study. Take time to think through how the study questions work together to accomplish that purpose. Second, the notes provide you with additional background information or comments on some of the questions. This information can be useful if people have difficulty understanding or answering a question. Third, the leader's notes can alert you to potential problems you may encounter during the study.

8. If you wish to remind yourself of anything mentioned in the leader's notes, make a note to yourself below that question in the study.

Leading the Study

1. Begin the study on time. Open with prayer, asking God to help you to understand and apply the passage.

2. Be sure that everyone in your group has a study guide. Encourage them to prepare for each discussion by working through the study questions.

3. At the beginning of your first time together, explain that these studies are meant to be discussions not lectures. Encourage the members of the group to participate. However, do not put pressure on those who may be hesitant to speak during the first few sessions.

4. Read the introductory paragraph at the beginning of the discussion. This will orient the group to the passage being studied.

5. Read the passage aloud if you are studying one chapter or less. You may choose to do this yourself, or someone else may read if he or she has been asked to do so prior to the study. Longer passages may occasionally be read in parts at different times during the study.

6. As you begin to ask the questions in the guide, keep several things in mind. First, the questions are designed to be used just as they are written. If you wish, you may simply read them aloud to the group. Or you may prefer to express them in your own words. However, unnecessary rewording of the questions is not recommended.

Second, the questions are intended to guide the group toward understanding and applying the *main idea* of the passage. The author of the guide has stated his or her view of this central idea in the *purpose* of the study in the leader's notes. You should try to understand how the passage expresses this idea and how the study questions work together to lead the group in that direction.

There may be times when it is appropriate to deviate from the study guide. For example, a question may have already been answered. If so, move on to the next question. Or someone may raise an important question not covered in the guide. Take time to discuss it! The important thing is to use discretion. There may be many routes you can travel to reach the goal of the study. But the easiest route is usually the one the author has suggested.

7. Avoid answering your own questions. If necessary, repeat or rephrase them until they are clearly understood. An eager group quickly becomes passive and silent if they think the leader will do most of the talking.

8. Don't be afraid of silence. People may need time to think about the question before formulating their answers.

9. Don't be content with just one answer. Ask, "What do the rest of you think?" or "Anything else?" until several people have answered the question.

10. Acknowledge all contributions. Try to be affirming whenever possible. Never reject an answer. If it is clearly wrong, ask, "Which verse led you to that conclusion?" or again, "What do the rest of you think?"

11. Don't expect every answer to be addressed to you, even though this may happen at first. As group members become more at ease, they will begin to truly interact with each other. This is one sign of a healthy discussion.

12. Don't be afraid of controversy. It can be very stimulating. If you don't resolve an issue completely, don't be frustrated. Move on and keep it in mind for later. A subsequent study may solve the problem.

13. Stick to the passage under consideration. It should be the source for answering the questions. Discourage the group from unnecessary cross-referencing. Likewise, stick to the subject and avoid going off on tangents.

14. Periodically summarize what the *group* has said about the passage. This gives continuity to the study. But don't preach.

15. Conclude your time together with conversational prayer. Be sure to ask God's help to apply those things which you learned in the study.

16. End on time.

Many more suggestions and helps are found in *Leading Bible Discussions* (IVP). Reading and studying through that would be well worth your time.

Components of Small Groups

A healthy small group should do more than study the Bible. There are four components you should consider as you structure your time together.

Nurture. Being a part of a small group should be a nurturing and edifying experience. You should grow in your knowledge and love of God and each other. If we are to properly love God, we must know and keep his commandments (Jn 14:15). That is why Bible study should be a foundational part of your small group. But you can be nurtured by other things as well. You can memorize Scripture, read and discuss a book, or occasionally listen to a tape of a good speaker.

Community. Most people have a need for close friendships. Your small group can be an excellent place to cultivate them. Allow time for informal interaction before and after the study. Have a time of sharing during the meeting. Do fun things together as a group, such as a potluck supper or a picnic. Have someone bring refreshments to the meeting. Be creative!

Worship. A portion of your time together can be spent in worship and prayer. Praise God together for who he is. Thank him for what he has done and is doing in your lives and in the world. Pray for each other's needs. Ask God to help you to apply what you have learned. Sing hymns together.

Mission. Many small groups decide to work together in some form of outreach. This can be a practical way of applying what you have learned. You can host a series of evangelistic discussions for your friends or neighbors. You can visit people at a home for the elderly. Help a widow with cleaning or repair jobs around her home. Such projects can transform your group.

For a detailed discussion of the nature and function of small groups, read *Small Group Leaders' Handbook* or *Good Things Come in Small Groups* (IVP).

General Suggestions

It is important that you work through the questions in each study from beginning to end. The questions were written to help you discover Matthew's main point. If only half the questions for a study are covered, it will be difficult to understand what Matthew intends to convey.

In order to cover the questions in a 45-55 minute study, firm leadership is very important. You will need to keep the group moving and not allow people to fix on any one question for too long.

Part 1: Discovering the King. Matthew 1:1—16:20.
Study 1. Discovering the King. Matthew 1:1—16:20.

Purpose: To consider how Jesus discloses his identity to us as the Son of God and true King of Israel, and to learn what it means to follow a heavenly King.

This study is a survey. It exposes people to Matthew's style and helps them catch a glimpse of his purpose. Help people not to be overwhelmed by the material they will cover. Encourage skimming and page flipping while looking for the obvious. In-depth study will come later.

Question 2. Matthew's theme is discipleship. He records Jesus' command to make disciples of the nations, "teaching them to obey everything I have commanded you." In his Gospel he gives us the commands and information necessary to make disciples. He, more then any other Gospel writer, gives us the content of what Jesus taught.

Question 3. Along with discipleship, Matthew wants us to see Jesus as the heavenly King who rules us. Beginning in Matthew 2 there is a repeated emphasis on kingship— the royal authority of Jesus. Also unique to Matthew is the emphasis on the kingdom of heaven, as opposed to the kingdom of God recorded by Mark and Luke. Matthew helps us see that Jesus' spiritual authority is supreme in all areas of life.

Question 8. Some people only think of conversion as a decision at a specific point in time. Help them think about the work of God which brought them to their point of commitment.

Study 2. In Search of the King. Matthew 1—2.

Purpose: To show that because Jesus comes as the heavenly King, everyone must respond to him—either in worship or rejection.

Question 2. It is clear that Matthew is not giving an exhaustive genealogy. He is more interested in showing significant relationships.

The lineage is important for several reasons. First, it establishes Jesus' royal lineage as the rightful King of Israel. Second, it shows his Jewish lineage. Being a son of David,

Jesus is qualified to be the Jewish King. As a son of Abraham, Jesus is indisputably Jewish. (Contrast with Herod who was only half-Jewish and not of a royal line.) Third, the lineage shows how Jesus fulfills prophecy as the anointed King sent from God.

Notice that several women are mentioned in the lineage. In light of the Great Commission at the end of the book it is significant that several of the women were not of Jewish descent.

Question 3. Jesus' supernatural birth and his divine nature are set forth clearly in these verses.

Question 4. The contrasts between Jesus and Herod are striking. Jesus was completely Jewish; Herod was of a mixed race. Jesus was sent by God; Herod was placed on the throne by the Romans. Jesus was to be shepherd of Israel; Herod was an exploiter of Israel. Herod took the lives of children to keep his throne; Jesus gave up his life so that the throne might be given to him. Herod "occupied" the Jewish capitol; Jesus was born in King David's city (and so on).

Question 5. Notice that Jesus is not welcomed by the established authorities of the Jewish world; he is welcomed by the foreign Magi. The religious leaders did not seek out the place of Jesus' birth and were not looking to welcome him.

Question 6. Help group members recall ways in which an interest in God has affected the books they have read, the friends they have chosen and so on.

Question 8. Herod was the first of many authority figures who wished to kill Jesus. Not being a full-blooded Jew, he had reason to fear one "born King of the Jews."

Study 3. Preparing for the King. Matthew 3:1-17.

Purpose: To see that in order to receive the King, we must prepare our hearts and be willing to turn from sin.

Question 2. John's ministry was modeled after Elijah's. In 2 Kings 1:8 Elijah is described as wearing a garment of hair and a leather belt. In Malachi 4:8 the one who is to prepare the way for the coming of the Lord is called the prophet Elijah.

Question 3. Israel wandered for forty years in the desert because of unbelief. Yet in the desert they learned to trust God enough to follow him into the Promised Land. Ministering in the desert, John the Baptist delivers judgment on the unbelieving religious leaders and offers the blessings of forgiveness to those who feel their need.

Question 4. To be a son of Abraham meant that one belonged to God and the promises of the covenant. The religious leaders were depending on their heritage for their relationship with God instead of cultivating a personal knowledge of God.

Question 5. Help people consider whether they may be depending on their religious affiliation or some previous commitment they might have made to the Lord. God wants a present and vital relationship with each of us.

Question 7. While John's baptism of water was outward and symbolic, Jesus' baptism was one of actual power. It would bring judgment on the unrepentant and a harvest of blessing to the responsive.

Question 8. John knew that his baptism was a form of divine judgment opening a door of divine forgiveness. John had trouble with the idea of bringing a baptism of judgment on God's righteous Messiah.

Question 9. Jesus' desire to receive baptism at the hands of John displayed his willingness to identify with the sins of the Jewish nation and to receive judgment from God. At the outset of his ministry it foreshadows the cross as the means by which he would fulfill his mission.

Question 10. The entire Trinity is involved at this crucial beginning point of Jesus' ministry.

Question 11. The mystery of the kingdom is that the Christ who has come is coming. We need to examine our lives to see that they are bearing fruit and not chaff.

Study 4. The Beginning of the Kingdom. Matthew 4:1-25.

Purpose: To catch the excitement of being invited to join Jesus' compassionate and powerful kingdom.

After the people have waited over a thousand years, the Messiah finally comes. It would be hard to grasp the excitement and anticipation present at the beginning of Jesus' ministry.

Question 2. Refer to a map of Israel. Zebulon, Nepthali and Galilee are in the northern part of Israel; Syria and the Decapolis are beyond the borders of Israel; Jerusalem and Judea are in southern Israel.

Questions 3-4. Commentators have noticed that Jesus is tempted in areas of humanity's greatest needs: sustenance, security and significance.

Satan appears to be questioning Jesus' identity as the Son of God. (Notice the repetition of the word *if* in verses 6 and 7.) However, the Greek construction used assumes the truth of the questions being asked. In essence, Satan is saying, *"Since* you are the Son of God. . ." He is tempting Jesus to use his position as God's Son in a way that violates God's will.

Question 6. Jesus is to be a light to the Gentiles, again foreshadowing the Great Commission. His ministry is one of preaching; the essence of his message was repentance in preparation for the kingdom of heaven.

Matthew emphasizes that Jesus' message was about the kingdom of heaven, in contrast to Mark and Luke who write of the kingdom of God. This difference has puzzled commentators for centuries. We suggest Matthew wanted to emphasize that Jesus' kingdom was of a spiritual nature and would continue when he ascended to heaven. Jesus now rules us on earth from his heavenly throne.

Question 7. A kingdom consists of a king with authority, subjects over whom he rules and the power to defend his realm. In these verses we see Jesus as an authority figure with authority to call followers (citizens) and the power to deliver his people from sickness and evil spirits. He is portrayed as the King from heaven who brings healing, compassion and deliverance.

Question 8. This is a key concept, central to the book of Matthew. Discipleship is following Jesus Christ. This simple definition needs to be considered closely. First, discipleship is personal—that is, it is being in a relationship with the person Jesus Christ. We are not called into a program of instruction. Second, our relationship with

Jesus takes priority over everything else: family, vocation and so on. Third, discipleship produces a transformation. Jesus promised to redirect them from fishing for fish to fishing for men. Fourth, discipleship has a mission focus. He requires that we learn to care for others so that we can bring them into a discipling relationship.

Study 5. The Law of the King (Part 1). Matthew 5:1—6:18.

Purpose: To learn how the Law of Jesus reaches into our hearts and requires total obedience.

Question 2. The first four beatitudes seem to concern needs: *The poor*—no resources. *Those who mourn*—a loss of some kind. *The meek*—no influence. *Those who hunger and thirst for righteousness*—a need for holiness.

Three of the remaining four beatitudes deal with conflicts: the merciful show kindness toward the undeserving. The peacemakers seek to resolve conflict. Those who are persecuted suffer oppression.

Question 4. The images of salt and light continue the theme that discipleship has an impact on others. It is important to note that the effects on society are the result of disciples who possess the qualities set forth in the beatitudes.

Question 10. In chapter 6 the focus is not on traditions and the Law but on motives and "acts of righteousness."

Question 11. The inner life is one of the main themes of the Sermon on the Mount. God is concerned with "heart responses."

Question 12. Jesus has high expectations of us. There is a sense of "firmness" in his character that comes out in the Sermon. Jesus also displays insight into human behavior: he knows what motivates us.

Study 6. The Law of the King (Part 2). Matthew 6:19—7:29.

Purpose: To count the cost and blessings of obeying the King's laws.

Question 2. The issue here, as in much of the Sermon on the Mount (and the kingdom of heaven), is one of motives and inner desires.

Question 3. The Old English word for worry meant "to gnaw at the neck like a wolf chewing on its prey."

Question 5. Judgment implies legal authority to decide a person's guilt or innocence. When we "judge" others we are rendering a decision about how righteous or unrighteous they are. This is a prerogative that belongs only to God. In discernment we are not rendering a legal judgment. Discernment is understanding the present disposition of others and acting accordingly.

Question 7. As you look at these specific verses, consider the way Jesus portrays the Father's character throughout the Sermon.

Question 9. Jesus stresses that our conduct must be in harmony with our claims. He does not recognize those whose lives contradict what they claim to believe.

Study 7. The Powers of the King. Matthew 8:1—9:34.

Purpose: To see the power of the King and to learn to please him by growing in faith.

These two chapters are a collection of the miracles Jesus did. The majority of the miracles which Matthew records are in these chapters. For this reason they form a unity. Matthew has organized the miracles to show that Jesus, as the King of the kingdom of heaven, has authority over everything and everyone.

These chapters also emphasize faith. The word *faith* is used repeatedly. Faith is the proper response to the authority of the King. Faith allows us to receive his authority and opens the knowledge of the kingdom to us.

Question 3. This incident displays the power and compassion of Jesus. Lepers were excluded from all social contact. The man is obviously desperate as he violates Jewish laws to approach Jesus in the midst of a crowd. To touch a leper in Jewish society was to become unclean. However, when Jesus touches the leprous man, instead of becoming unclean, he makes the leprous man clean.

Question 7. The fury of the storm and the depth of their fear is evident when we consider that the disciples were seasoned fishermen and had sailed on the lake all their lives. Yet after having displayed his power through the working of miracles, Jesus expected his disciples to understand how powerful he was and who he was. Once again the kingdom demands a response of faith in Jesus.

Question 8. Jesus' display of power over the violent men was terrifying, and his sending the pigs into the water seriously damaged the town's economy.

Question 9. Genuine miracles serve to authenticate the claims of the one who performs the miracles. Others have done supernatural healing—for example, Elisha and the apostles—but they have not claimed to be God's Son or to have the authority to forgive sins.

Question 10. As a doctor Jesus brings spiritual health to those sick with sin. As a bridegroom he brings celebration to those who love him. The parables of wine and new cloth mean that his ministry cannot be patched with old traditions or contained by traditional restraints (vv. 16-17). The emphasis is on distinctiveness. The kingdom Jesus brings is new and distinct.

Study 8. The Messengers of the King. Matthew 9:35—11:30.

Purpose: To see that we must count both the cost and the blessings of being the King's messengers.

Remember that the theme of discipleship runs throughout Matthew. In this section we see the disciples as they are being transformed into fishers of men. Jesus has modeled the ministry of the kingdom and now sends them out to put into practice what they have seen him do.

Question 3. The disciples are being sent out as representatives of the kingdom of heaven. The peace they will offer to people is not just a wish for well-being and good fortune. Rather it is the gift of spiritual peace and right standing in the sight of heaven. The rejection of the peace the disciples offer has eternal consequences. For this reason it was important that they physically display the consequences of their actions by shaking the dust off their feet in response to rejection.

Question 6. The central issue in discipleship is the priority of Jesus. Remember that the disciples had to leave their family and vocation in order to follow the Lord.

Question 8. While John had prepared the way for Jesus, his faith was wavering. Jesus was not meeting John's expectations of the Messiah. After all, John was still in prison when he expected to be delivered by the conquering Messiah. Jesus offered concrete evidence that he is in fact the Messiah and performed messianic acts as prophesied in Isaiah 61.

Chapter 11 continues a theme begun in chapter 10. We see the consequences of those who have heard of Jesus and have refused to respond.

Question 10. Jesus' denunciations must be seen in light of the mission of the twelve disciples. They had gone throughout the nation proclaiming the kingdom, healing people and casting out demons. Despite both Jesus' and the disciples' ministry, people in those cities still refused to believe.

Study 9. The Leaders and the King. Matthew 12:1-50.

Purpose: To feel the security of belonging to the King as we see Jesus handle opposition with wisdom and power.

The opposition to Jesus which had been slowly building now becomes open conflict. As the religious leaders seek to oppose him, Jesus confronts them with the serious consequences of their actions.

Question 3. If the religious establishment could demonstrate that the Law supported their teaching, then they could prove that Jesus was not sent from God. On the other hand, if Jesus could demonstrate that they had not understood the Law correctly, then his authority would be established and the religious leaders discredited.

Question 4. Meeting personal needs and serving God are not forbidden on the Sabbath. Implicit in Jesus' answer is a claim of his own divinity. The disciples were with him and were doing his will.

Question 5. While Jesus is healing on the sabbath, the religious leaders are plotting murder.

Question 6. Jesus saw the Law as a means of serving people. The Pharisees saw people as servants of the Law. In Jesus' hands the Law became a means of deliverance. In the hands of the Pharisees it became a means of control.

Question 7. The contrast between God's attitude as recorded by Isaiah and the religious leaders is striking:

God	Religious Leaders
Chosen	Rejected
Beloved	Hated
A delight	A thorn
Just	Unjust

Question 8. The accusation that Jesus served Satan was the second prong of the Pharisees' attack on Jesus. If the Pharisees could convince people that Jesus was demonic, then everything he did and taught would be considered evil.

The sin against the Holy Spirit is unforgivable because it is a deliberate choice of spiritual darkness over light, and hardness over responsiveness. It is the Spirit that brings light and a responsive heart. When we call the work of the Holy Spirit evil, then there is no avenue left open for God to work in us. By attributing the work of Jesus to the evil spirit as opposed to the Holy Spirit, the religious leaders were putting themselves in danger of complete darkness.

Question 9. As a follow-up question, you may wish to also ask: "How is Jesus greater than either Jonah or Solomon?"

The extent of evil that religious leaders are committing is illustrated as Jesus compares them with Gentiles who were willing to repent when confronted with God's judgment.

Study 10. The Parables of the King. Matthew 13:1-58.

Purpose: To learn that only through sincere interest can we understand the mystery of Jesus' kingdom.

There are a variety of definitions of a parable. For our purposes we will define a parable as a story which illustrates the message of the kingdom of heaven. This is a lot of material to cover in one study, but there are benefits from doing so. When we look at all the parables here in one setting, we can begin to see the common theme of the growth of the kingdom of heaven.

Studying the parables requires sober judgment. Many people are inclined to become fanciful in their interpretations. The best way to avoid error when studying them is to look for the one main point in each parable.

It is also important to keep in mind that an interpretation of a parable must be done in context. Check to see if the interpretation fits with the questions being asked and with the issues under consideration.

Question 2. Remember that the theme of Jesus' message was that the kingdom of heaven is at hand—in other words, Jesus, the One sent from heaven, is here to bring God's rule. The parables illustrate the way Jesus' authority is active in the world.

Question 3. Don't allow the discussion of this parable to be sidetracked with the question of "eternal security." The issue is not whether everyone who responds to the preaching of the Word is eternally secure. Rather, it is that there are a variety of responses to the gospel, not all of which are truly genuine.

This parable is frequently called the parable of the sower. It could easily be called the parable of the soils. The difference between responses depends on the varying quality of the soil. The soils picture the quality of our hearts as they respond to Jesus' message. Matthew continues to emphasize inner responses to Jesus in his Gospel. The opposition to growth could be described as the world, the flesh and the devil. The devil takes up the seed from the heart, the flesh does not persevere in times of tribulation, and the world creates such temptation that the seed becomes choked.

Question 4. Remember that Jesus is now speaking to a crowd that has been infected with opposition from the religious leaders. Jesus must now teach in such a way as to elicit the interest of those who are spiritually hungry but confused by the false teaching about him. The mystery of a parable is revealed to those who are interested enough to ask questions when they don't understand. It is hidden from those who are not spiritually interested and hungry.

Question 5. The growth of the kingdom is mysterious. Until the end of the age it has a mixed character, and not everyone who appears to be a member of the kingdom really is. Who really is and is not a member of the kingdom will not be made known until the consummation of the kingdom at Christ's Second Coming.

However, this is not a parable which forbids church discipline, as some might imagine. The field is the world, not the church. Those who might prematurely pull up weeds are not other Christians ("sons of the kingdom") but the divine servants, probably angels.

Question 6. The kingdom of heaven is also mysterious because of the way it began. It started off so much smaller then expected. Instead of coming with a conquering army, Jesus chose twelve disciples. And instead of setting up a separate political order, he sent his disciples as salt into the world or as yeast working throughout the dough.

Study 11. The Revelation of the King (Part 1). Matthew 14:1-36.

Purpose: To see how Jesus uses our experiences to bring us spiritual insight.

Question 2. Herod had been hearing about the works of Jesus. This question provides an opportunity to reflect on what Matthew has said about the mighty works of Jesus up to this point, particularly in chapters 8 and 9.

Question 3. Again, this question must be answered in light of previous study in Matthew. The disciples are called to exercise faith based on all they have learned from being with Jesus and through ministering in his name.

Question 5. Knowing that John's death at the hands of Herod was a foreshadowing of his own, Jesus steps up the training of the disciples.

Question 8. The significance of the disciples' confession (v. 33) can only be under-stood against the background of their Jewish heritage. God's holiness was so jealously protected that many refused even to pronounce God's name.

Study 12. The Revelation of the King (Part 2). Matthew 15:1—16:20.

Purpose: To see that our understanding Jesus' identity is the central issue of the kingdom of heaven.

This is another long study because Matthew gives us crucial details that lead up to the great confession of Peter.

Question 3. The escalating conflict with the religious leaders continues in these two chapters. At this point the issue of who really is faithful to the law is settled. The tradition of Corban, allowing someone to declare money or a piece of property as devoted to God and then give it as a gift to be used in the temple, appeared holy. In reality it allowed people to avoid family obligations for religious advancement and social prestige.

Question 5. The central issue of these chapters is *insight,* looking past outward acts to the truth. This gentile woman approaches Jesus as the Jewish King, the "Son of David." She receives help from Jesus when she moves past his apparent rejection. Seeing her faith and insight, Jesus grants her request. Matthew puts this incident here to show us that Jesus would expect the same type of insight from his disciples.

Question 7. Jesus refuses to do a sign because the religious leaders were too blind to see the true meaning of his works. In effect, it was not possible for them to receive a sign from heaven.

Question 8. The disciples were looking only at the outward and obvious meaning of Jesus. This was also the problem of the religious leaders.

Question 9. Peter is given spiritual insight by divine relation from the Father. The faith to perceive that Jesus is the Christ, the Son of God, is not natural; it is supernatural.

Part 2: The Rejection and Resurrection of the King. Matthew 16:21—28:20.
Study 1. The Conflict and Victory of the King. Matthew 16:21—28:20.
Purpose: To survey the conflict and cost the kingdom requires of Jesus and us.

This study, like the first one, is a survey. Remember not to let people become overwhelmed by the amount of material that will be covered. Encourage skimming and page flipping. Look for obvious points. Move people along, and don't let the discussion focus for too long on any one question. It is important for the group to get through the whole survey.

In this survey you will see a continued escalation of the conflict and tension between Jesus and the religious leaders. The cross which Jesus declares to Peter in Matthew 16:21 is discernible just behind the scenes in each chapter. In the midst of this growing conflict Jesus faithfully instructs his disciples. Another theme that continues to build in this half of Matthew is the authority of Jesus. Much of the action takes place in Jerusalem, from chapter 21 onward, in and around the temple. The King enters his capital city which is controlled by rebels. The final victory of the King comes, not as he expels the rebels, but as he submits to them, is killed and raised to life by the Father. In the final earthly scene he declares that the kingdom of heaven is indeed at hand and that all authority in heaven and on earth has been given to him.

Study 2. The Work of the King. Matthew 16:21—17:27.
Purpose: To learn that living by faith means we may not always understand; nevertheless, we must trust and obey.

Question 3. Jesus' predictions must have been hard for the disciples to believe for several reasons. First, it would be unthinkable that the Messiah should die before establishing his kingdom. Second, it would be incomprehensible that the religious leaders could actually kill God's Messiah. (It is ironic that Jesus' enemies are the leaders of Israel rather then the heathen oppressors.)

Question 4. It is possible that Satan was speaking through Peter. Or it may be that Jesus used *Satan* as a figure of speech to show the terrible implications of trying to revise the true purpose of his mission.

Question 5. Jesus reveals the true cost of discipleship. We must not only place him first by leaving everything, we must also place our lives in his hands. The cross is an instrument of death, like a hanging noose in the old West. Jesus is saying that we must be ready to die, even to the point of carrying our own rope so that we can be hung!

Question 6. *The Son of Man* refers to a bright shining figure in Daniel 7:14 who comes from heaven at the end of time to judge the nations and to set up a kingdom that will never be destroyed.

The mystery of the kingdom of heaven is that it is present in the person of Jesus. When the disciples see Jesus revealed in all his glory as the Son of Man, they are seeing Jesus as he truly is, the King of the kingdom of heaven. In light of Jesus' shattering prediction of his death, it was important for them to know that death was not the end.

Question 7. Moses and Elijah may represent the two major divisions of the Old Testament, the Law and the Prophets. God appeared to Israel in a cloud as he led the nation through the wilderness.

Question 8. Malachi prophesied that Elijah would return before the final judgment. Jesus sees a present and future role for Elijah, preceding Jesus' First and Second Comings.

Study 3. Life in the Kingdom (Part 1). Matthew 18:1-35.

Purpose: To discover some of the values Jesus requires as we live in his kingdom.

Jesus continues to instruct his disciples. There are similarities between this material and the Sermon on the Mount. In the Sermon on the Mount Jesus teaches the essentials of discipleship to those who have just begun to follow him. In chapters 18—20 Jesus prepares to physically leave them in order to lead them from heaven. He tells them what they will need to know in order to lead the church.

The central theme of these three chapters is "Who is the greatest in the kingdom of heaven?" It begins in 18:1 and continues through 20:20-28, when the mother of James and John requests positions of honor for them.

Question 3. Concerning the topic of children, most people assume that Jesus is encouraging trust, openness and innocence. However, the main point concerning children is that they have little social status; we don't naturally think of children as being "great." Jesus teaches that positions of greatness in the kingdom are not to be calculated according to traditional understanding of social status.

Question 5. These verses emphasize Matthew's concern to teach about disciplemaking. We will be held accountable for the quality of our lives and our teaching.

Question 6. These verses also address the issue of making disciples. God wants to bring lost sheep to himself. Disciples who are following the Lord will share his concern for those who are lost.

Question 8. Quality relationships are a central issue in the kingdom of heaven. Jesus provides ways for us to handle our conflicts with one another and to resolve them.

Study 4. Life in the Kingdom (Part 2). Matthew 19:1—20:34.

Purpose: To see how the values of the kingdom conflict with the world's approach to wealth and leadership.

Question 2. Help the group to see that Jesus' teaching on divorce and remarriage reflects important kingdom values such as commitment, faithfulness, forgiveness, humility, submission to God and so on.

Question 4. The young man claimed that he had kept all the commandments. However, his response to Jesus indicates that he loved his wealth more than he loved God. Therefore, he was guilty of breaking the first, second and tenth commandments (see Ex 20:1-17). Jesus lovingly exposed the man's true condition.

Question 6. We are to live expectantly, looking forward to the abundant and eternal provisions of the kingdom. Our present earthly position may not correspond to our future eternal position (v. 30). However, verse 29 promises what every Christian has experienced to some degree: when we follow Jesus we become part of a worldwide family and benefit from the hospitality, gifts and care of other Christians throughout the world.

Question 7. God is free to give us what he chooses; he owes us nothing for any of our labor. Any amount he pays us is an expression of grace.

Question 9. Jesus' teaching stands the world's concept of authority and greatness on its head. Those who have many servants are not great, but those who serve many.

Study 5. The King Occupies His Capital. Matthew 21:1-27.
Purpose: To observe the rising conflict in Jerusalem over Jesus' authority and how it reveals the difference between genuine faith and empty profession.

The central issue in this passage is the authority of Jesus. As he enters Jerusalem, his conflict with the religious leaders reaches a boiling point. As the King sent to bring the rule of heaven, Jesus goes to the temple where he should receive the prayer and praise of God's people. Instead, he must drive out those who are busy making a worldly profit.

Question 4. Some saw Jesus as the King who would free the Jewish nation from oppression and then rule over them forever. Others saw Jesus as a prophet. However, most Jews would not equate the Son of David with a prophet.

Question 6. The temple was to be a place of compassion and health for the needy and a place of praise and prayer to God.

Question 7. Jesus was looking for the fruit of prayer and faith. He curses the fig tree to illustrate to the disciples what the true condition of Israel is like. Israel is on the brink of withering because of their rejection of him.

What is required of the disciples is that they learn the relationship between prayer and faith. Jesus instructs the disciples on faith because that is the central issue in the conflict. The religious leaders refuse to believe and their place of worship has degenerated into a place of commerce.

Question 8. Remember that the religious leaders have been saying that Jesus is a lawbreaker and gets his power from Satan (Mt 12). They are no longer trying to discredit him with the crowds. They are looking for ways to trap him and bring him to trial.

Study 6. The King Silences the Opposition. Matthew 21:28—22:46.
Purpose: To consider the dangers of rejecting Jesus' invitations.

The conflict between Jesus and the religious leaders continues. However, instead of rejecting and avoiding them, he continues to meet with them and reach out to them in their blindness through hard-hitting parables. As we observe Jesus in this conflict we can learn more about the character of our Lord and what he requires of us as his disciples.

Question 4. It is always good to examine our responsiveness to the Lord. Remember that the religious leaders had convinced themselves that they were doing God's will. We also are in danger of deluding ourselves that we are obeying God when we may be just serving our own interests.

Question 5. Among other charges, Jesus is accusing the religious leaders of being guilty of his death.

Question 7. To side with either would have taken the focus off God and put it on man.

Question 11. In this paragraph we glimpse the mystery of the kingdom of heaven. Christ is both eternal and yet born. He is a son of David and yet the Lord of David. He is born in time but is above time.

Question 12. Jesus is a firm assertive Lord who does not bow to opposition out of weakness. We can trust him to protect us and draw strength from his strength.

Study 7. The King Condemns the Rebels. Matthew 23:1-39.

Purpose: To consider the commands and demands that Jesus makes of opponents and followers.

In this chapter Jesus delivers the final judgment on the religious leaders. There are seven woes. The number seven has biblical significance: it means complete and full. After this chapter Jesus will have nothing more to say to the religious leaders. Their rejection of Jesus is total and results in their condemnation by Jesus.

Question 6. As you look over the woes, remember that these are more then just an emotional outburst. This is the final word of the King personally delivered to the rebels.

Question 7. The religious leaders' influence would prevent many from believing.

Question 8. Think of ways that personal acts of piety can degenerate into rituals that have lost their meaning. Or how traditions in the church which may have once been full of meaning can become rituals that no longer result in obedience to God.

Question 9. Remember that as the religious leaders condemn Christ they are condemning their Lord and Creator. They rejected God after having the most personal encounter with him that anyone in the history of the world ever experienced!

Question 11. He expressed a longing for them. In sending the prophets, wise men and teachers, he had given them many opportunities to repent.

Study 8. The Return of the King. Matthew 24:1-51.

Purpose: To consider the importance of perseverance and of living in anticipation of the King's return.

This chapter has been abused and misused. People who want a blueprint for the future miss the primary focus and value of Christ's words. Jesus clearly indicates that everything in heaven and earth will pass away—except those who are related to him, who believe and obey his word.

It will not be possible to explore the depth of this passage nor many of the issues it raises. Keep in mind that the central focus is the return of Christ. Now that Jesus has condemned the religious leaders and they have determined to kill him, Jesus must prepare the disciples for his final victory on the cross and his return from heaven.

Question 2. The temple represented the presence of God. As long as the temple was standing, every Israelite believed that God was present with his people.

Question 4. Jesus warns us that the events referred to in verses 4-8 are not the primary signs of his coming. They have happened throughout history.

Question 6. It is not clear from the text when the abomination that causes desolation will take place. Commentators differ on whether it took place in A.D. 70 or whether it is to take place in the future just prior to Christ's Second Coming (see 2 Thess 2:1-12). Early Christians thought it referred to their time and fled Jerusalem prior to its destruction by the Romans. Some believe it was given as a warning both for the early Christians and for those living at the time of Christ's return.

Question 7. Many commentators believe the events referred to in verses 15-25 focus primarily on the fall of Jerusalem at the hands of the Romans in A.D. 70. But it is possible that Jesus had more than just the Roman conquest in mind.

Question 9. Jesus' return will be visible to all and not secret. In some way his return will have to do with the skies. Lightning, vultures and celestial bodies can be seen by anyone looking at the sky.

Study 9. Preparation for the King's Return. Matthew 25:1-46.
Purpose: To consider the ways Jesus holds us accountable for our actions until he returns.

Now that Jesus has told the disciples he is leaving them for a while, he tells them how they must live until he returns. The thrust of the parables is that we must live in constant expectation and in consistent obedience.

Question 2. The point of the parable of the ten virgins is that Jesus wants us to be prepared and to live in anticipation of his return. Don't be sidetracked by a discussion of eternal security.

Question 4. The genuine disciple of Jesus is responsible for the resources given to him or her. Jesus did not judge people for the amount of return, but for the lack of initiative and investment.

Question 7. It is common to interpret the parable of the sheep and goats simply in terms of the hungry, the sick and those in prison. In this view, entrance into the kingdom will be based solely on one's treatment of the poor and oppressed. Some have even claimed that the parable abolishes all distinctions between Christians and non-Christians since anyone who is benevolent will gain access into the kingdom.

The proper interpretation of the parable hinges not only on the treatment of the sheep and goats, but also on the identity of Jesus' "brothers." It is very possible that Jesus' brothers refer to his disciples (see especially 12:48-49; 23:8; 28:10). The fate of the nations will be determined by how they respond to Jesus' followers, those who are charged with spreading the gospel and do so in the face of hunger, thirst, illness and imprisonment. Good deeds done to Jesus' followers, even the least of them, are not only works of compassion and morality, but reflect where people stand in relation to the kingdom and Jesus himself.

Study 10. The Betrayal of the King. Matthew 26:1-75.

Purpose: To observe what Jesus and the disciples teach us about how to respond to temptations and trials—and how not to respond.

The plot against Jesus is consummated in chapters 26 and 27. In this study we see Jesus submit to the schemes of religious leaders for the sake of his mission. Help the group to observe the wide variety of actions and emotions: the terrible treachery of Judas and the tender compassion of Mary, the touching intimacy of the Last Supper and painful apathy of Gethsemane, the passion of Jesus in the garden and his resigned passiveness at his trial.

Question 3. It is ominous because Jesus speaks of his death. It is hopeful because he speaks of drinking with them again in the kingdom. How confused the disciples must have been!

Question 8. In verses 15-16 Judas makes himself available; he can be bought. Yet strangely his actions are part of the divine plan.

Question 10. There are at least two reasons for Jesus' silence: his mission is to die, and his accusers are not interested in the truth.

Question 11. The immediate effect of Jesus' statement is to make the chief priest furious. However, the ultimate effect will be that Jesus, as judge of the world, will be the final judge of his accusers. Jesus is alluding to Daniel 7:14 when the Son of Man will come at the end of the age to judge everyone.

Question 12. Peter believes in Jesus so he wants to be near Jesus in his distress. His fear of death however is stronger than his faith at this point in his life.

Question 13. Encourage the group to recall what happened in the Garden of Gethsemane. In preparation for his trials, Jesus prayed. In spite of Jesus' warnings (vv. 31, 40-41), the disciples slept. How might prayer (or the lack of it) have affected their responses to temptation and trial?

Study 11. The Crucifixion of the King. Matthew 27:1-66.

Purpose: To consider the mysterious triumph of the kingdom of heaven through the suffering and death of Jesus on the cross.

This is a grim chapter. Jesus is killed. It appears that evil will triumph. Both the international authorities (the Romans) and the local authorities (the Jewish leaders) participate in Jesus' death. You may discover that there is a sense of letdown as you finish the study. This is to be expected. We all need to look at the terrible reality of the death of Jesus at the hands of humanity. After you finish the study, encourage people to look forward to the last chapter on the resurrection.

Question 7. There was a split in the Godhead which affected all of creation.

Question 9. Most of Jesus' followers were not present. However, the women watched from a distance. Joseph was also courageous in asking for the body of Jesus. Some of the emotions they might have felt were sadness, responsibility, loyalty, love, care, pain and so on.

Study 12. The Resurrection of the King. Matthew 28:1-20.

Purpose: To consider why the resurrection of Christ is a victory we can't keep quiet about.

The confusing mystery of the kingdom of heaven takes on new clarity as Jesus returns from the grave. While Jesus physically leaves them, he becomes more present then ever as he ascends to heaven. On the foundation of Jesus' life, death and resurrection the disciples can truly become fishers of men—as he promised would happen when he called them.

Question 5. The religious leaders have been given the final sign promised them in Matthew 16:1-4: the sign of Jonah. Jesus has been in the grave and has risen. But as has been evident all along, the religious leaders are not open to the work of God and are only interested in preserving their power and social status.

Question 8. How would the disciples have gotten by the Roman guard in order to steal the body? The penalty for sleeping on duty was death. Even if the guard did fall asleep, how would the disciples get past a sleeping guard and move the large gravestone that blocked the cave without waking them?

Question 11. When the birth of Jesus was promised, he was called Immanuel, God with us. As the Gospel of Matthew ends, that is what Jesus has become. By his ascent to heaven he also remains spiritually with his people in all places and at all times. The conclusion of the Gospel is the same as it was at the beginning: "Repent, for the kingdom of heaven is near!"

Stephen Eyre is a training specialist with InterVarsity Christian Fellowship for the southeast United States. He is the author of Defeating the Dragons of the World *(IVP). He and his wife, Jacalyn, have had extensive experience in Bible study groups.*